THE EAGLE
AND
THE RIVER

CHARLES CRAIGHEAD

photographs by
TOM MANGELSEN

Macmillan Publishing Company
New York

Maxwell Macmillan Canada
Toronto

Maxwell Macmillan International
New York   Oxford   Singapore   Sydney

To my father, Dr. Frank Craighead, Jr.
— C. C.

Text copyright © 1994 by Charles Craighead. Illustrations copyright © 1994 by Thomas Mangelsen.
All rights reserved. No part of this book may be reproduced or transmitted in any form or by any means, electronic
or mechanical, including photocopying, recording, or by any information storage and retrieval system, without per-
mission in writing from the Publisher. Macmillan Publishing Company is part of the Maxwell Communication
Group of Companies. Macmillan Publishing Company, 866 Third Avenue, New York, NY 10022.
Maxwell Macmillan Canada, Inc., 1200 Eglinton Avenue East, Suite 200, Don Mills, Ontario M3C 3N1.
First edition. Printed in Hong Kong by South China Printing Company (1988) Ltd.

2 4 6 8 10 9 7 5 3 1

The text of this book is set in 14 point Palatino. Book design by Constance Ftera.

Library of Congress Cataloging-in-Publication Data
Craighead, Charles.
    The eagle and the river / by Charles Craighead ; photographed by Tom Mangelsen. — 1st ed.
        p.   cm.
    ISBN 0-02-762265-7
        1. Stream fauna—Snake River (Wyo.-Wash.)—Juvenile literature.
2. Bald eagle—Snake River (Wyo.-Wash.)—Juvenile literature.
3. Snake River (Wyo.-Wash.)—Juvenile literature. I. Mangelsen, Thomas D., ill. II. Title.
QL215.C73   1994
591.5′26323′097961—dc20   92-23240
Summary: An Eagle flies over a wintry landscape, looking for fish in Idaho's Snake River and watching
the other animals that inhabit the area.

In the clear, cold winter air of Wyoming, a bald eagle soars in lazy circles high above the land. The trees are bare and still. Except for the Snake River, a twisting ribbon of dark water flowing swiftly through a white landscape, the frozen land is covered with snow.

From the vantage point of the eagle it is easy to see why this winding river was named the Snake. It twists and turns and never flows in a straight line. The river's banks are made of loose rocks and sand left by a glacier, and each spring the flooding river washes away parts of its banks and makes new paths. Sometimes it takes shortcuts, and sometimes it makes a wide loop around a place where tree roots hold the soil together.

As it flies, the bald eagle looks down into the Snake River for fish to catch. During the warm summer, the river was kept full by snow that continued to melt in the mountains, and fish moved from one deep pool to another looking for insects floating on top of the water. The fish were fat and easy to catch when they swam to the surface to eat. But by fall most of the mountain snow melts and the river gets lower and lower. In some places it becomes only a trickle between one deep spot and the next. When the weather turns cold, the shallow water freezes easily and many flying insects die. The fish eat very little and stay in deep pools where the eagle cannot see them. On some winter days, the eagle does not eat anything.

The eagle flies lower, looking into the shallow water. Here the Snake River is broken into many small river channels, which are braided together like a rope. When one path of the river changes during the spring floods, trees in the new path are washed away, and plants soon grow in places the river used to flow. A channel that once cut through a stand of old spruce trees may soon sprout grass and cottonwood trees. This makes a mix of old and new trees, grass, willow thickets, and open meadows.

The more kinds of plants there are in a place, the more different types of animals can find food and shelter there. With their mix of plants, the braided paths of the Snake River are home to many animals, especially in winter when the river is one of the few things moving in the still and frozen world.

The bald eagle rests from its hunt for fish and lands in its favorite cottonwood tree. From there, the eagle can see up and down the river. Even though it is the middle of winter and the landscape seems lifeless, the eagle's sharp eyes find life everywhere.

A small herd of elk paw at the snow near the river's edge in search of dried grasses. In the summer lush grasses grow along the moist riverbanks, providing winter grazing for the herd.

Nearby, a family of mule deer stands in the thick brush growing near an old river channel. They dig in the snow to uncover small plants and nibble at the tender ends of twigs. In spring the deer will leave the river and go high into the mountains.

Out along the edge of the river, the eagle sees a small gray bird running along the ice and diving boldly into the cold water. This is the dipper. Swimming to the bottom of the river and holding on with its claws, it looks for insects to eat. The dipper has warm, oily feathers that shed water and flaps that cover its nostrils so water cannot get in. In the summer the dipper lives in fast mountain streams. When the streams freeze, the dipper finds a winter home on the Snake River.

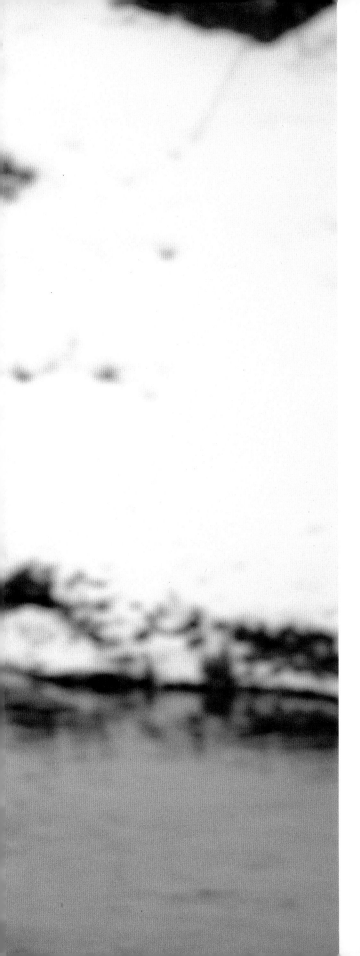

The bald eagle can spot fish swimming in the river, but even with its sharp eyes, it cannot see all the life moving under the surface when winter freezes the world above. Many of the summer's flying insects lay their eggs in the river, where they hatch into wingless larvae called nymphs. The nymphs live underwater all winter and are the main food of the fish and dipper bird. In the warmth of spring and summer, the nymphs will emerge from the river, shed their nymph skin, and become adult flying insects. They will mate, lay eggs in the river, and die, completing their life cycle.

Out in the current the eagle sees a small flock of ducks bobbing in the water. These are mergansers, ducks that catch small fish underwater.

Closer to shore, goldeneye ducks dive for plants and insects. While the world above is cold and frozen, the underwater world continues to provide food for the animals that survive near the Snake River.

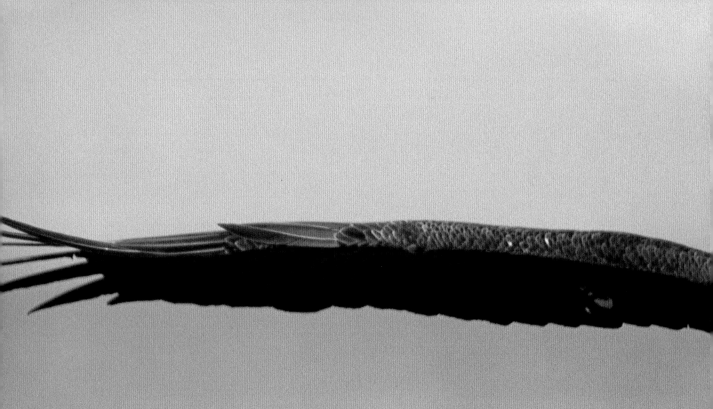

Suddenly, the eagle spots the swirling movement of a fish in the river. Lifting its broad wings, it glides out of the tree in a steep dive, but just as it reaches out with its powerful talons, the fish swims quickly into deeper water. Circling, the eagle watches the water, and then flies away up the river.

From the air the eagle sees the tracks of an animal going in a long line along the edge of the river. The tracks, leading from place to place, tell the story of the animal's travels as it explored brush piles and snowdrifts. Far upriver the eagle sees the animal that made the tracks. It is a coyote, hunting near the river. Sometimes the coyote will surprise a river-dwelling animal, such as a muskrat or beaver, near the shore, but mostly it catches mice or finds animals that have starved or frozen to death.

As it glides along, the eagle sees a small white flash darting in and out of the snowbanks. This is an ermine, a white weasel that catches mice under the snow. It is pure white except for its eyes and nose and the tip of its tail. In summer the ermine sheds its white fur and grows brown fur, blending in with the new season's natural colors. Through the summer it is called a weasel, but in the fall it once more changes into a beautiful white ermine.

  Landing on a dead snag, the eagle again watches the river. A loud commotion in the willows makes it turn its head and watch. Three black-and-white magpies are flitting up and down through the branches as they squabble over a piece of food. Their black wing feathers glisten in the sunlight. Their long tails help the birds stay balanced as they chase each other about. Like the coyote, magpies are good scavengers and clean up whatever the eagles, otters, and other hunters leave behind on the shores of the river.

Along the river's edge, just below the eagle's tree, are the signs of a nocturnal animal usually seen just as it is getting dark: gnawed sticks and trails leading through the snow to trees that have been cut down. At the riverbank are piles of sticks with the bark chewed off. Right on the bank, next to deep water, is a big pile of sticks and mud. This is the lodge of the river beaver. There is a secret underwater tunnel leading from the river to a dry room hidden in the middle of the lodge. Beavers need deep water for protection and in order to swim in search of food, so they usually build dams to make ponds. Instead, the river beaver uses the flowing Snake River as its home and has no need to build a dam. It is no different from other beavers except for its choice of home. All winter the beavers eat the bark of trees and willows growing along the river.

The bald eagle is hungry and once more flies off in search of fish. As it circles high above the river, it sees something swish in the water. The eagle gets ready to swoop down and catch a fish. Instead of a fish, however, the dark head of a river otter appears, followed by another, and another. Soon there are four otters swimming and diving in the water. The otters live by catching fish. They are also playful animals that love to slide on the ice and snow. Their thick fur keeps them warm. Sometimes when the otters catch a fish and take it out on the shore to eat, the eagle swoops down and scares them away long enough to grab the fish. But now the otters are not fishing.

Below the eagle, a large black bird glides silently out of the trees and lands on a large piece of driftwood near the river's edge. It puffs up its feathers and gives a loud, coarse call. This is the raven, one of the smartest and most adaptable birds in the world. The raven lives near the Snake River all winter. Like its cousin the magpie, the raven is mostly a scavenger, but it is also a good hunter.

On the water below the eagle are two white shapes like soft icebergs. As the shapes gracefully turn, the eagle sees the long, curved necks and black bills of rare trumpeter swans. The swans come to the river when their favorite shallow ponds freeze. As they swim along, they reach down with their long necks to find plants and seeds on the bottom.

A sudden splash in the water alerts the bald eagle to a fish feeding near the surface. In one graceful move the eagle turns and swoops down. Gliding just above the water, it reaches out with its powerful feet and sharp talons, and snatches the fish out of the river. With a few strong flaps of its wings, the eagle flies up and lands in a tree to eat the fish. Then, full of food and ready for a cold night, it drops the remains of the fish to the ground where a coyote, magpie, or raven will soon find it.

The eagle puffs out its feathers for warmth, and as night comes, all the land seems frozen and quiet. But the eagle hears the Snake River gurgle under the ice and sees the beaver slip out of its stick lodge to swim across the river for a dinner of willow bark. The dipper pops up out of the icy water with a last billful of insects. A moose and calf come to the river for a drink and then disappear back into the brush.

The Snake River with all its wildlife is home to the bald eagle. From its roost it watches nighttime come over the land, and as it gets darker and darker, it hears the slap of the beaver's tail, the howl of the coyote, and the deep hooting of the great horned owl that hunts the riverbanks by night. Fog forms in the cold night air. The last thing the eagle sees before falling asleep is the faint reflection of twinkling stars in the moving, living Snake River.